CW01636646

ANTHO

The Manager's CODE

First published by 6JA Publishing 2022

First edition

ISBN: 978-1-8380062-2-8

This book was professionally typeset on Reedsy. Find out more at reedsy.com

To my wife, Jo, the best man-manager I've ever met!

Contents

Foreword

Anthony has done it again.

He has simplified and codified the key to effective line-management, making this book a must-have in any line manager toolkit.

Recognising the change in the cultural landscape of our post-pandemic era, this book ensures line managers will not only consistently achieve business results but they will achieve them in the right way. The book shines a light on all that is wonderful about leading and managing a team and demystifies the art that is people management.

A highly practical guide that when followed will make a difference to all line managers, and another great read from Anthony Taylor.

Jo Wright,

CEO Coaching Culture

Preface

I wrote this book for the same reason I've spent the last ten years as a leadership coach and facilitator, and that's to do what I can to end the scourge of poor management behaviour.

In my twenty years as an employee in many different companies and industries I had the privilege to work with some fantastic managers. The kind of people you'd walk through walls for. Who would inspire you and make you love coming into work. I also worked for the other kind. The ones who could ruin your week just by turning up in the morning. The ones who left your confidence in the gutter and your stress levels in the clouds.

I don't believe for a second that, all bar the four percent who are statistically psychopaths, (yes they walk among us) they meant to be that bad. It's just that they probably hadn't been shown a better way and that's how they were managed and so the cycle continues.

My aim with this book is to, at least in some small way, change that cycle and help managers, at whatever level but especially those starting out, practice the four simple habits they can do to be great managers.

I'm not one for long-winded reads, lord knows I've wasted hours of my life reading books that could have been condensed into a quarter of their length. This is why this book is short and sweet. Get in, get out, get on with your life. Just please, actually do something different as a result of reading it.

Acknowledgement

No man is an island, they say. And so it is with this book. It would be impossible to list everyone who has had such a positive influence on me. But in some small way, those that have over the years, have contributed to this book being written. To all of you, thank you.

Even to those of you who were some of the worst managers I've ever had or heard about, thank you. I've learned as much about how not to do it from you as from the good ones.

1

Praise for The Manager's CODE

"I love this book. It distils the information, advice, models and reasoning I wish I'd been given 15 years ago into an easy to read, digestible and practical guide." - Russ Parfit, Training & Development Manager, New Look

"Love CODE. Really easy to remember - keeps it simple and each section is broken down efficiently to unpack all the information and guidance. With this book I was able to read it in one sitting. It's the perfect length and the way it flows made it easy for me to go back in to pick up on key points. Chapter summaries and questions work really well and the examples and nods to other authors add further credibility. Really enjoyed it." - Daniel Finn, Learning & Development Specialist at Vodaphone.

"I loved this book. It's informative and a good read. I specifically liked the summary and key takeaway points, along with the questions at the end of each section." - Catherine McGaw-Pratt, Global Learning and Development Manager at Infosys Consulting, Inc.

2

Introduction

It's an exciting challenge managing people and leading a team. It's also a huge privilege. Not only are you responsible for the performance of the individuals and collective team, but you hold within your power the ability to exert a significant influence on the lives of those people.

It's these interpersonal relationships that are the biggest driver of workplace well-being. As they impact well being so much, we can be sure that they significantly impact performance since unhappy people don't perform to anything like their potential.

Just take a moment to think about your experience to date. Who are the great managers you've had? What was the difference they made to you in your engagement, well-being, and performance at work and outside of work? Did you find yourself feeling confident? Walking taller?

Now compare that to some of the poorer managers you've had. How did they make you feel? How engaged did you feel? Did they get the best out of you? What about your confidence and happiness? Did it have an impact outside of work? Were you less patient with those at home? Did it impact your sleep?

Research conducted in 2018 tells us that 86% of an employee's job satisfaction is attributable to their relationship with management, according to Jan De Neve of the Oxford Research Center.[1]

Research worldwide shows that people often cite having a poor manager as their number one reason for leaving a job ahead of the company.

A poll of over one million workers in the U.S. by Gallup found that leaving a bad manager was the number one reason workers quit, with 75% of those who left voluntarily doing so because of their boss and not the job itself.[2]

The relationship with a direct line manager is critical to several employee success factors, including productivity, morale and engagement. But a breakdown of that relationship, for whatever reason, can lead to mistrust, anxiety and job dissatisfaction. A more recent study released this year by CareerAddict of 1,000 workers found that 79% would consider lousy leadership as a factor in deciding to quit.[3] Four in ten went so far as to say they would return to their old job if their former boss was replaced.

But you are not like those bad bosses, are you? Or are you?

There's something called the Dunning Kruger effect, which is a cognitive bias whereby people with low ability in a task overestimate their ability.[4] We tend to overrate ourselves because we do not see the qualitative difference between our performances and the performances of others. It can lead us to make bad decisions, such as engaging in behaviour dangerous for ourselves or others due to being unaware of or lacking the necessary skills. It may also inhibit us from admitting our shortcomings to ourselves.

We might think that training is the answer. It could be, yet it's often done poorly, or the individual motivation behind attending is so weak that it means little changes.

In 2019 more than $370billion was spent globally on training, yet the most significant cause for concern amongst learning and development teams was the effectiveness of the training.[5]

In that same year, according to the OECD (Organisation for Economic Co-operation and Development), the U.K. had an estimated 2.4 million untrained 'accidental managers'.[6] These tend to be people who are what I call 'battlefield promotions'. These are managers who have been promoted to mid-ranking positions on the mistaken assumption that being good at a specific job makes them a good manager, and many have had no formal development training.

For example, a manager leaves, and someone from within the team is promoted, often without regard for whether they are the best person for the job. Usually, it goes to whoever is best *at* the position. They may have lots of skill in an area only matched by their level of unconscious incompetence. They don't know what they don't know. I was one of those people early in my career.

This leads to poor management behaviours and practices, decreasing engagement, performance and well-being. Then when those people become managers, they often mimic the style they experienced because they've not been shown a different way, a better way.

For the last few decades, businesses have been, to some extent, able to tolerate this. The industrial revolution meant the focus has often been on processes and systems. However, the new age of technology and information is driving the need for better, more inclusive and collaborative management practices. The globalisation of markets, knowledge, and culture means that managers and companies compete against each other like never before.

One of the battlegrounds is the war for talent. Along with technology, the culture of the younger generations is changing. Millennials, those born between 1980 and the late 1990s, and Generation Z, those that follow them, are driving a cultural change in the workplace.

Many are re-evaluating what they want from work, and re-shaping the psychological contract between employer and employee. It's not enough anymore to work just for the paycheck; they want to feel fulfilled. Perhaps you do too.

The Covid pandemic is also changing attitudes. The mental health impact felt by many forced into working from home, led by managers lacking the basic skills of effective management and driven by demands from above to deliver operational targets, has led to what many are calling the Great Resignation.

According to a Mind Share Partners survey, two-thirds of millennials who left their jobs in 2021 cited mental health reasons, and the proportion for Generation Z was even higher, at 81%.[7]

Employees are re-evaluating their career and life aspirations and weighing these up against how their employer and managers have treated them, and deciding to vote with their feet.

The fact that many businesses learned that they could operate profitably in a hybrid model, coupled with an increasing desire among workers to work that way, means that there will be an even more significant premium on effective managers. As Marshall Goldsmith said: "The ability to get greater results and preserve well-being amidst change and challenge, is the defining skill set of our times."

I'm going to assume that as you are reading this book, you are at least interested in and open-minded enough to admit that perhaps you don't know everything and want to work on your management skills. This book aims to equip you with the knowledge and tools to implement what I've identified as great managers' four key behaviours or habits.

It's what I call the CODE.

3

What is Management?

IT'S NOT THIS

Look up 'What is management' in Oxford Languages Dictionary, and it says:

1. The process of dealing with or controlling things or people
2. (Archaic) Trickery; deceit

It is perhaps not surprising that many people have had such a poor management experience when we look at it through that lens.

Of course, that's not the only definition of management; there are countless others, many of which offer a more positive view of what it is. A better one of those is:

Management is the process of guiding the development, maintenance, and allocation of resources to attain organisational goals.

That strikes me as being a much more holistic yet not necessarily people-centred approach to management. That said, the word 'guiding' is essential here. It fundamentally differs from the word 'controlling' offered in the first definition.

Legendary management thinker Peter Drucker has been described as the father of modern management practice. You may have already come across some of his work in training courses. He was an Austrian who fled the Nazis and settled first in England and then in the United States in 1937.

Drucker believed that the only way to prevent the second coming of fascism was to create a "functioning society," the cornerstone of which, he said, was strong institutions – including corporations, which he believed had a duty to be as virtuous as they were profitable.

Management practised well, was Drucker's protection against evil. While we might not be fighting fascism, lousy management practices can ruin careers, destroy confidence, damage well-being, and significantly impact the bottom line.

THE FIVE FUNCTIONS OF A MANAGER

Given that Peter Drucker is so highly regarded and his management theories have stood the test of time, it's worth briefly looking at what he believes are the five functions of a manager.

#1 Setting Objectives & Planning

- To determine the objectives aligned with the corporate vision and mission statement
- To determine the goals in each area of objectives
- To decide what has to be done to reach the objectives
- To communicate the goals to the people whose performance is needed to attain them

#2 Organising the Group

- To analyse the activities, decisions, and relations needed
- To classify the work
- To divide the work into manageable activities and further divide the activities into manageable jobs
- To group units and jobs into an organisation structure
- To select people for the management of the units and for the job to be done

#3 Motivating & Communicating

- To make the team out of the people that are responsible for various jobs
- To empower employees and motivate them to follow through on your strategic focus
- To take relationship responsibility
- To make decisions on pay, placement, and promotion
- To communicate constantly to and with subordinates, superiors, and colleagues

#4 Measuring Performance

- To establish yardsticks and the factors that are as important to the performance of the organisation and every man in it
- To make the measurements focused on the performance of the whole organisation and every individual available to each staff member
- To analyse, appraise, and interpret performance
- To communicate the meaning of the measurements and their findings to your subordinates, to his superiors, and colleagues

#5 Developing People

- To develop yourself
- To develop others

WHAT NOBODY TELLS YOU ABOUT MANAGEMENT

That list from Peter Drucker is a pretty comprehensive assessment of things a manager is responsible for and supposed to do, but it's not what management boils down to, and it's not what this book is about. What nobody tells you about management is that it is really about people. Sure, processes and data matters but behind all of that are people.

Yet most managers get little or no formal training in managing people. And as anyone who has managed people for any length of time will tell you, people can be complicated to manage, primarily when they are managed poorly from the outset.

Darcy Willson-Rymer is the CEO of Card Factory in the UK and former

CEO of Starbucks UK. He said, "As you climb the ladder, you must identify the learning curve you have. What is the technological learning curve you have and the leadership behaviour curve you have? Make sure you spend more time on the leadership stuff. It's the leadership behaviours that will make you successful."[8]

Being an effective manager boils down to two things, and these are the only two things that are your responsibility and what you are measured against:

1. Achieve the expected results
2. Keep your team engaged and developing. That's it.

DELIVER EXPECTED RESULTS

While this is simple to understand and read, it's not always that simple to do. One of the biggest reasons I've seen in over twenty years of management is the simple lack of clarity about expectations.

Try this out on yourself for a moment. Can you list off the top of your head the five most important results you are expected to achieve this quarter or year? Do you know what they are for your team? Do your team know what they are?

If not, why not? If you can't, I strongly suggest you think about what you believe they are and then sit down with your boss and check with them. If they don't match up, don't leave until you are crystal clear about them.

Nothing costs organisations and individual managers more dearly than people running around focusing on the wrong things.

ENGAGE & RETAIN YOUR PEOPLE

The next thing that costs businesses dearly is disengaged people and high staff turnover. The cost of replacing an individual employee can range from one-half to two times the employee's annual salary — and that's a conservative estimate. In the U.K. staff turnover runs at about 15%, and in the U.S. it's about 23%. So, a 100-person organisation that provides an average salary of $50,000 could have turnover and replacement costs of approximately $660,000 to $2.6 million per year.[9]

Well-run businesses monitor staff retention rates, and they keep an eye on managers who seem to be bleeding staff at a higher rate than others. Based on just the accepted numbers we've seen, one manager can effectively wipe out any profit his team generates in staff turnover costs.

In addition, there is a war for talent that the pandemic of 2020/1 has exacerbated. People are re-evaluating their priorities and reflecting on how their companies and their managers treated them. It's called the Great Resignation, as many mid-career workers leave or plan to leave their jobs within the next six months.[10] They aren't just quitting and walking away but shopping around to find a better fit between values and work-life balance.

The manager that can engage and keep their staff will set themselves apart from the competition. The rest of this book will show you four habits essential to do that.

CHAPTER SUMMARY

Key takeaways:

Much is written about management and the many functions a manager has to fulfil, and they are distilled into two responsibilities: Get the required results and retain your good people.

When it comes to deciding whom to promote and who moves ahead in their career, it's the manager with a proven track record in both of these areas that gets the nod.

Technical ability isn't enough; the people development bit makes the difference. Willson-Rymer adds, "Don't hold someone else back because of your anxieties, insecurities or career aspirations, because it will eventually backfire."

Great managers are people-focused first and foremost.

The most significant influence on the engagement of your people at work is your relationship with them.

Questions to Reflect On

1. How focused are you on your people instead of yourself or other things?
2. How good is your relationship with them? Would they agree? How

do you know?

3. What areas might you want to work on?
4. How will you identify these and measure progress?

4

How to be a great manager

SKILLS V QUALITIES

What makes a great manager? It's a question I thought a lot about when I was working in the corporate world and I've asked many clients and delegates on my programmes over the last decade. And, it's a question that generates much debate and a wide variety of answers. Is it about skills or qualities?

When I ask, a selection of typical answers includes things like:

- A good people person
- They are good at listening
- Everyone likes them
- They are clever and don't get flustered
- They seem to have all the answers
- They are well respected
- They've gained a good reputation

- They are goal orientated and focused
- They create trust

Yet, what if a manager wasn't meeting his targets and was failing to retain his people? Would they still be considered a great manager? I hope we agree the answer is not. What is required is a blend of both skills and qualities.

Given that technical skills and required qualities will vary substantially across industries and roles, what I've done is codify the behavioural habits of effective managers regardless of industry.

ALL POWER IS NOT CREATED EQUAL

One of the most significant barriers managers have to creating the high-performing team they would like is using the wrong type of power. I was guilty of this during my career. More so, perhaps because I didn't know better at the start. Later on, it was borne out of my inability to manage my emotions better in some circumstances. I allowed frustration and impatience to get the better of me.

Every manager possesses two types of power: position power and influence.

POSITION POWER

Position power is pretty self-explanatory. The position of being a manager comes with a certain amount of authority. The manager must get things done through other people, which comes with the ability to tell them what to do.

There may be consequences if a direct report doesn't do what is asked. We've all been told to do things that we either didn't want to do or didn't agree with, and we did them anyway. Why? Position power.

The problem is that it's the least effective of the two types of power. Think back on your own experience. Who was a manager that you came across that relied on position power? How did that make you feel and respond?

Position power is like a heavy broadsword. It smashes, cleaves and is cumbersome. It's heavy to wield and is tiring.

INFLUENCE

Influence is the second kind of power a manager has at their disposal. This is more challenging to accrue and develop but is considerably more beneficial when getting things done and building high performing teams.

Influence encourages discretionary effort. It generates intrinsic motivation in others which is always more powerful than the extrinsic motivation of position power.

There have been many books on influence and how to generate it. Study them. Apply what you learn. The payoff will be worth it.

Influence is like a Samurai sword. It takes time to create; it's razor-sharp, more robust than you might think, light and easy to wield to significant effect with minimal effort.

Reflect on your experience to date. Which manager have you had or heard about that had great influence? What did they do to build that influence, and more importantly, how did they choose to wield it?

THE C.O.D.E.

Being a great manager isn't rocket science. It's about doing the basics well. The four habits transcend industries, roles and experience. If every manager did these four things consistently and consistently well, they would boost productivity and staff engagement whilst reducing staff turnover.

There are four behaviours or habits that I've identified and called the C.O.D.E., which stands for

Connect Observe Deputise Empower

When you practice these four habits, your influence will grow significantly. The more influence you have, the higher performer you are likely to be and the higher-performing your team will be.

Each is a habit at a macro level, a behaviour driven by a mindset or a management and leadership philosophy. At the micro-level sits the skill of applying the habit. I'll provide a model for each skill.

Each of these models is not the only way of applying that skill; you may have your own. They are, however, what I have found to be highly effective. Much of their effectiveness lies in their simplicity.

The simpler something is, the more likely we will apply it consistently. The more consistently we use it, the more effective it becomes. Think about MacDonalds for a moment. What separated them from every other fast-food outlet was the simplicity and consistency of their process, which meant that a customer had the same experience (burger) regardless of whether they were in California or New York.

They set the standard that revolutionised the food industry.

Reflect on your own experience for a moment. Have you ever worked for or with someone whose attitude or behaviour was as changeable as the weather? How did that impact you? How does that compare with someone who behaves consistently?

CHAPTER SUMMARY

Key takeaways:

1. What makes a great manager is not what most people think it is
2. There are two types of power: position power and influence
3. Spend time building influence and use position power sparingly
4. There are four habits that all great managers do consistently
5. They are: connect, observe, deputise and empower

Questions to Reflect On

1. Which kind of power am I using the most?
2. How is this helping or hindering my team and me?
3. How consistent are my behaviours?

5

Connect

"I'm only as successful as my weakest team member."

– Adam Massman, Executive Director, Head of Global Learning & Leadership Development at JLL

WHY CONNECTION?

Quite simply, because human beings are hard-wired for connection, we have had to work together to survive over the course of human evolution. We needed to collaborate to find food, shelter,warmth, security and more. Some social anthropologists believe that homosapiens prevailed over the bigger, stronger and bigger brained neanderthals because we learned to collaborate better. That allowed for faster technological development and bigger tribe sizes.

Abraham Maslow realised this when he published his hierarchy of needs.[11] His triangle put love and belonging as the third most important factor after physiological and safety requirements. This has been brought sharply and painfully into focus with the global pandemic of 2020/21.

Many of us found ourselves isolated in our own homes, disconnected from friends, family and work. It's no coincidence that during this time, poor mental health increased. Indeed in his book Lost Connections – why you're depressed and how to find hope, Johann Hari and his research identified that disconnection from nine key things drove depression and not, as many believe, a chemical imbalance.

What has that got to do with a book on being a great manager? Two of those disconnections were from other people and meaningful work, and a third was status and respect. Have you ever worked somewhere where you felt you didn't fit in and you weren't treated fairly or with respect? How did you feel? How engaged were you? Did you do your best work?

THE BEST CONNECTION MODEL

As I've said before, none of the four habits is rocket science. None are difficult either, but most are done surprisingly badly by many people. When it comes to connection, I will share with you a simple yet highly effective model to build a relationship. It's so simple that I'm guessing most people will discount it. They'll make excuses like, "I do this already", "My team don't want to do this", or perhaps the most common,"I don't have time".

If you find yourself saying one of these or something similar, humour me and stick with it. Try it as I outline it for three months, and if you and your team members don't see a benefit, then go back to what you were doing. Oh, and feel free to email me and tell me. I'm confident you won't need to.

The best way to build a connection is to meet weekly and have a one-to-one. That's it. How *consistently* you do this and *how you do this* make the difference. Why? I'm guessing most of you reading this have some close relationships, whether that's with a partner, spouse, child or close friends. Now imagine ignoring them for a few weeks. Not totally, but all your conversations are purely transactional. "Have you put the bins out? Have you paid the gas bill? What do you want for tea? Have you done your homework? etc."

If all your interactions were purely transactional in nature, how do you think that would impact your relationships? Do you think your spouse would be more or less open to amorous intentions? I'm guessing less. Do you think your children would be more or less interested in spending time with you? What about your friends?

Do you know people that just talk about themselves and aren't interested in you? How does that make you feel about them?

If we want our relationships to be fulfilling and rewarding, we need to show an interest in the other person. We need to find out how they are and what's going on for them. What are their concerns, fears, joys and victories? You get out what you put in. It's no different at work. If we want discretionary effort from our people, we need to put in the time to build a connection.

A great way to think about it is the emotional bank account – you may have heard of that term. When we proactively do things that build trust, we make deposits into the account. When we do things that decrease trust, we withdraw on the account. Things that build trust include: taking time to listen and understand, empathy, supporting development, praising good work, constructive and fair feedback, being fair, being consistent, being self-aware, apologising etc.

Actions that decrease trust include: being inconsistent in mood and behaviour, destructive feedback, being unfair, not listening, talking too much, telling too much, being unsupportive etc.

Think about one person you manage. How full or not is your emotional bank account with them? How well do you know them? Can you name their spouse and children or those closest to them? If not, I'd argue you don't know them well enough. If you can't be bothered to know the names of the people most important to them, why should you expect their discretionary effort?

HOW TO DO WEEKLY 1-2-1S WELL

Like baking a cake, a weekly one-to-one done well requires specific ingredients in the correct order and baked for the right amount of time. I'll lay out these steps below. You can download a free PDF copy of the effective one to one cheat sheet from my website.[12]

SCHEDULE

The key to these is to have them weekly and ideally at the same time every week. That consistency allows you to manage your diary and time better. Most importantly, it sends a message to that person that they matter. Do this consistently; by that, I mean >85% success rate, and your emotional bank account with them will hold more than the Federal Reserve.

I know, I can already hear you protest that you don't have time, and you speak with your team every day. That's not the same, and it's not as effective and not what you'll be doing.

To start, take a look at your calendar. I'm guessing the next two weeks are pretty full. Three weeks from now, less so, and it's largely empty after that. The best way to do this is to ask your direct report to choose a time in your calendar at least three weeks from now that works for both of you and schedule the 30min meeting. Ask them to make this a weekly recurring appointment not to be missed. It's better to avoid either straight before or after known occasions like staff meetings, board meetings and your meetings with your boss. You do have those, right? Oh, and don't choose a Monday morning; most of us move and think as fast as a tortoise on a Monday morning, and don't choose a Friday afternoon as most of us have checked out by that point.

Explain why you are asking them to book these in. By asking them to do it, you are making them part of this commitment and giving them a say in when this will occur. You are building a connection and trust.

AGENDA – 30MINS

The key to any successful meeting is to start with a clear agenda and time frame. In your weekly meetings, this couldn't be more simple. It begins with 15mins for them and 15mins for you.

They always go first. This shows respect and builds trust. Seek first to understand what's going on for them before being understood. Besides, when we talk, we only learn what we know; we might learn something new when we listen.

Make it clear that their time is their opportunity to talk about whatever they want. It can be work-related, it can be home related, it can be about the weather if they want. But. When their time is up, that's it. It's your turn.

You can get to talk about whatever you want. Primarily, managers choose to talk about work-related stuff – updates, organisational news, priorities etc. It's also your chance to ask them questions that can help you improve performance, remove blockages etc. All the things as a manager you'll be interested in.

Questions that you might choose to ask could include:

What are your biggest time wasters/frustrations? What do you see as being your biggest priorities? What do you need from me over the week or two? Would you like more or less direction from me? Is there anything you are hung up on? What do you need to do your job more effectively?

There are eight other questions to consider on the cheat sheet.

You might also ask them about their goals and personal development plans.

When your fifteen minutes is up, the meeting ends. It's critical that your timekeeping is on-point for several reasons. It respects both of your valuable time. It focuses the mind on the most important thing for each of you to bring up, and it means that you are both more likely to keep to future meetings.

We've all been in poorly run meetings where we have lost hours of our lives to them. We've learned to avoid them like the plague. Don't allow your meetings to become like those.

The only caveat to that is if your direct report brings up a mental health issue. Then, it's essential that you give them as much time as is required.

LOCATION

When it comes to property, the saying is location, location, location. When it comes to having your meetings, location is also important. Having your meetings in a public place is a no-no. How likely is it that someone will feel relaxed enough to share personal insights etc? Is there a likelihood they will be overheard? Equally, fully private, while the ideal, isn't always required. Somewhere semi-private will do. Most workplaces are now open plan, so breakout areas and huddle spaces are sometimes an option.

With the move to hybrid working gathering pace since the pandemic, many meetings may have to be done virtually. Remember not to assume that the other person has complete privacy at their location. Check first.

On that note, while one-to-ones by phone are an option, video is preferable. I'd always suggest you start the call at the agreed time and be on time.

NOTETAKING

First and foremost, these meetings are business meetings and should be respected as such. You might consider me old-fashioned, but I think there is something important about taking notes, especially handwritten notes.

Firstly it shows the other person you are interested enough to bother. Secondly, it's a great way to keep an accurate record of what's discussed. Over time, especially when it comes to appraisal time, having a history of the content of conversations and showing general themes and progressions can be invaluable. I don't know about you, but I can't remember what I did last weekend, let alone the pertinent bits of a conversation six months ago!

I now use a reMarkable to capture my notes, but I still use the same layout as my paper notes. If you'd like a PDF copy of the paper version with 14 questions to ask as a prompt, then you download a copy from my website.

PREPARATION

I have an old friend who has risen the ranks in the Army; his favourite saying is "proper preparation prevents piss-poor performance" – the six Ps.

When it comes to preparing for the meeting, I used to find that an uninterrupted ten minutes would often be enough. During those ten minutes, I do four simple things:

- Consider their current priorities and projects
- Review last week's meeting notes
- Think about what needs following up and my aims for the meeting
- Consider what encouragement and positive feedback I can give

The preparation bit, even just ten minutes, is so important. If you do all the rest and don't do this, it can undermine your efforts. We've all been in meetings where it's as clear as day that someone hasn't prepared for it. How did that make you feel? What did it say about them? If it was a meeting with your manager, what did it tell you about how they valued you?

It goes back to building trust and an emotional bank account. If you come prepared, it shows you are genuinely interested in them, their development, their feelings etc. It says, "You matter." We all want to matter. That's not soft or touchy-feely. It's simple good manners and bloody good business sense.

You might get away with it from time to time, but only if you have some serious capital in the emotional bank account. You can rest assured that they will tell other colleagues if you make it standard practice either to be prepared or especially if you are unprepared. You have then unwittingly withdrawn from their bank account too.

SOMEONE GOOD DOES THIS

Adam Massman is a busy man. He is responsible for more than 80 people who deliver the entire global learning and development function to 100,000 colleagues at Jones Lang LaSalle, a commercial real estate business.

Adam has 15 direct reports spread around the world. With such a large and dispersed team, it would be understandable if Adam couldn't meet with them all regularly. However, this is not Adam's mindset. As I've outlined, he understands the importance of connection and making time for each person.

Adam meets every one of his team virtually, every Wednesday for 30mins. Every week, that entire day is given over to spending time with each person without fail. "It's an important time because building a connection builds trust. I need to trust my team, and they need to trust me," he says on our Zoom call.

Adam rarely, if ever, misses a day because he has set the expectation with his stakeholders that this is his time with his team. "I am very transparent with my stakeholders," he says. "In the past, I've had to spend time with stakeholders because something my team has done has not gone according to plan. They know that if I spend time with my team, it means issues like these are less likely to crop up."

Some managers see it as a waste of time. Not Adam. "It's my number one time-saver. By doing this consistently, I've got to a point where I hardly get emails from my team between meetings. We tackle things in those sessions, and they get on with it. It allows me to know what's happening in the trenches without being in the trenches."

By doing this, Adam is creating time for himself and self-reliant and capable colleagues. "It takes time," he adds. "It took two to three months before I started to see a return on the investment. You have to meet people where they are."

Adam also has something called 'office hours' on a Friday morning, where any of his team can contact him for a chat about anything that's on their minds. They rarely do, but it's there, and they know it.

CHAPTER SUMMARY

Key takeaways:

1. The weekly one-to-one is the foundational habit of great managers
2. It only takes 30 minutes and should not run over
3. Always take handwritten notes
4. Remember the Six Ps – preparation is key

Questions to Reflect On

1. What's stopping me from trying this?
2. How does this differ from my approach to one-to-ones?
3. How consistent am I with my one-to-ones?
4. Are they as effective as I would like?
5. Do I spend most of the time talking and telling?

6

Observe

"P*ositive reinforcement is one of the easiest and quickest ways to improve employee happiness and effectiveness."*

– The Disney Institute

WHY OBSERVATION?

As a manager,it's essential that you are abreast of what's happening with your team, especially when it comes to performance. Remember, the first priority of every manager is to get the expected results. Getting better than anticipated results would be ideal. So how can you do that, and how does observation fit in?

Think about your own experience for a moment. How often have your previous bosses spent more time on what's wrong and either repairing it or, worse still, punishing someone for it? Sure, as managers, we are paid to solve problems, but that doesn't mean it's us that have to solve them.

Most managers get sucked into a problem-focused mindset somewhere along the line, so that's all they see as a result. It becomes the focus of their communication with their teams. They spend their time asking questions like: "How did this happen? Who's fault is this? Who made this cock-up?" Do you agree?

And what's the result of this? I'd argue that to varying degrees, it promotes the growth of fear, worry, a blame culture, reduced psychological safety, stifled creativity, underperformance, impaired collaboration and discretionary effort.

Surely we want our teams to display the positive versions of those things. So how can we 'see' things differently?

Simple. Look for the positives more than we look for the negatives and when you see them, praise the behaviour. Barbara Frederickson, a Professor of Psychology, has done extensive research on the ratio of positivity to negativity. Her work suggests that a ratio of 3:1 is ideal.

This correlates with other work done by the Gottman Institute into the patterns of behaviour and interactions between happy and unhappy couples. Based on these alone, they have a proven track record of predicting with a 93 per cent accuracy which relationships will last and which will flounder.

It's the same story when it comes to parenting. The research is emphatic regarding the importance of praise to reinforce the kind of good behaviours we want to see in children. Neuroscience studies indicate that we respond to social approval in much the same way that we respond to monetary rewards (Bhangi and Delgado 2015). Praise feels good. And certain types of praise can lead to beneficial outcomes. So why do we not do that in the workplace?

Perhaps it's because we worry it will over-inflate egos. Maybe it's because we didn't get much, so we repeat our experiences. Perhaps it's because, as adults, we think we shouldn't need praise. Having a job and doing the job is reward enough, right?

Wrong.

We don't stop being human beings when we grow up, and just as we don't stop needing food, water and sleep, nor do we stop needing praise. Praise boosts confidence, increases motivation, builds resilience and promotes discretionary effort.

I'll give the final word on this to Darcy Willson-Rymer, "The other thing is never to underestimate the power of recognition. When people aren't successful and don't do a good job, 90% of the time, it's a failure of leadership, not a failure of the individual."[13]

Wouldn't you want more positive behaviours from your team? If you answered yes, then here's how to do it well.

THE 4-S FEEDBACK MODEL

The first step in using this model is to tell people what to expect. I recommend announcing it at a team meeting or, better yet, in your weekly one to one, which you'll be doing from now on, right?

Explain the purpose of feedback, which is to encourage effective future performance. Then walk them through the model. I like to explain it something like this: "I have an obligation to help you be at your best every day. Giving you real-time feedback is just a way for us to have that conversation consistently and without ambiguity about what you are doing and the results."

Then you only give positive feedback using this model for around eight weeks. Yes, eight weeks. Suppose you have to give negative feedback in that time, use another model or however you have been doing it. Although, hopefully, you haven't been using the old 'shit- sandwich technique. Have you?

Then after eight weeks or more, you can start introducing negative, but ideally constructive feedback, using the model.

We wait eight weeks because we don't want them to associate the model with negative feedback just yet. We need you and the model to build a big enough emotional bank account that future withdrawals don't put you in the red.

SEE

It all starts with observation and seeing the behaviours you want more of. Sadly, most managers wait too long before giving feedback. If a direct report does something either positive or negative in the morning, the classic response by a manager is to do nothing. Most will hope the person has realised what they have done wrong and self-corrected. They take this approach because they don't feel confident in challenging the behaviour.

Or if it's positive, they have the mindset that you can't go around praising good behaviour; it's just what people should be doing. It's just their job, and they are paid to do it.

Over to Darcy again: "Why thank the accounts payable person for processing 250 invoices in a day? Well, because it took a great effort and great skill on the part of that person to do their job, you should recognise them for that. It goes a long way, and it gets you much more engagement than pay."

So the average manager either leaves it until later because they lack confidence or don't see the value in praise. Either way, they often leave it till later to say something, if they do so at all. The problem with leaving it until later is that we can only talk about what's happened in the past. We can't change the past. It's much better to focus on the behaviours we want to see more of in the present.

SET-UP

Success is down to how something is set up like so many things in life. The comedian sets up the punchline; the goal scorer is given the pass that puts them through the defence, and the building stands on the foundation.

When it comes to feedback, the set-up begins with a simple question: "Can I give you some feedback?" or "Can I share an observation with you?"

It's essential to get their permission. In marketing, permission is everything. It massively increases the likelihood of a sale. In management, it massively increases the probability of receiving and listening to the message.

"What if they say no?" you ask. Then say "OK," and walk away.

Firstly, in my experience, not many people say no. You'll find this even less after you have been giving only positive feedback for eight weeks. If they do, and you walk away, here's what's most likely to happen. They'll be back inside 24 hours, asking what you were going to say.

Why? Because curiosity gets the better of them. As human beings, two things drive stress: a fear of losing approval and a perceived lack of control. The latter has three parts: the need to be correct, the need to be perfect and the need to know.

This last one means they are likely to be back at your door asking what it was you were going to say.

When you've got to this point, it's time for the third 'S'.

STATE

This has two parts: state the behaviour and state the impact of the behaviour. It's imperative you do both and in that order. At all times, we must stick to facts and not opinions. When we stick to facts, we can reduce ambiguity. Facts are indisputable. Opinions are vague, open to interpretation and create a grey area where conflict and entrenched positions live.

As my wife says: "Opinions are like arseholes; everyone has one. It doesn't mean you should get it out in public."

When it comes to stating the behaviour, it sounds like this:

Positive feedback

"When you… got the report to me early; it meant I could get the pack to the CEO early too, which makes us all look efficient. Thank you."

Negative feedback

"When you…didn't put the sign out on the wet floor, that means we are in breach of health and safety protocols. This puts residents at risk of injury and the business at risk of legal action and fines. It also means I have to keep checking on you, which I don't want to do."

Notice that the feedback begins with "When you…" in each case. It then describes the behaviour before explaining its impact, either positive or negative.

SOLUTION

When the feedback is positive, the fourth step is not needed. There is often nothing else to say but thank you or a "keep it up". After all, the purpose of giving feedback on positive behaviour is to encourage more of that behaviour.

However, when the feedback is negative, a solution is often needed. In this case, we are looking for a change of behaviour by way of a solution. The average manager jumps straight into 'tell' mode. That's counterproductive. It often escalates the perceived threat response in the person receiving the feedback, when they realise it's negative feedback. This is why it is vital first to build your emotional capital with someone.

A much better and less threatening way is to ask them a question. It might be something simple like:

"Can you change that? Can you remember next time, please?" Although these are OK, they are closed questions, eliciting a 'yes' or 'no' answer.

A better way is to make it an open question: "How can you remember next time?" or "What do you need from me to help you remember next time?"

This is what engages them in finding a solution. It encourages them to think about the issue and problem-solve for themselves. It stops learned helplessness, which is where people expect to be told every last thing, meaning you as the manager spend too much time fire-fighting and checking up rather than getting on with your work.

It also means they are more likely to follow through on the action they identified. A conscious decision not to do that creates cognitive dissonance, that awkward feeling we have when we have not done something we said we would do or behaved in a way we know is not correct.

If you think there is a genuine reason why their solution either won't work or can't be done, ask them what else they could do. This is where employing the fourth habit can help. Your last resort is to tell them the behaviour you want them to do.

If you find yourself giving advice too quickly, I suggest reading The Advice Trap – Be Humble, Stay Curious and Change The Way You Lead Forever by Michael Bungay Stanier.[14]

CHAPTER SUMMARY

Key takeaways:

1. The importance of feedback in behaviour change cannot be overestimated
2. Always ask permission to give feedback– respect their answer
3. Always state the behaviour and impact of behaviour factually
4. Stay away from opinions
5. Ask for their solution or say thank you

Questions to Reflect On

1. What's stopping me from trying this?
2. How does this differ from my current approach to giving feedback?
3. How consistent am I with giving both positive and negative

feedback?

4. What's my positive to negative ratio?
5. Do I ask for their solution or tell them mine first?

7

Deputise

"When *you delegate tasks, you create followers. When you delegate authority, you create leaders.*"
– Craig Groeschel, founder of Life Church

WHY DEPUTISE?

When I was a child, I used to love watching Westerns. One of my favourites is El Dorado with John Wayne, Robert Mitchum and James Caan. In the film, the three heroes are up against a much larger group of ruthless men and the Sheriff, played by Mitchum, deputises Wayne and Caan by simply throwing them a deputy sheriff badge.

He gave them the authority to help him achieve his objective of protecting the town and seeing off the bad guys. He knew he couldn't do it alone. He delegated.

Yet, so many managers I come across in business are reluctant to delegate. They don't know how, when or what to delegate, which is seriously holding them and their teams back from achieving the results they want.

As part of the research for this book, I spoke to over 200 managers across multiple industries and countries and of varying degrees of experience. Time and time again, people said delegation was critical for things like: "upskilling and confidence building", "delegation drives empowerment and team development", "allows people to stretch and grow and sometimes fail", "creates a sense of self-worth in people when done correctly", "demonstrates high levels of trust and encourages ownership of issues creating a positive working environment".

My favourite response was this: "without delegation (1) you cannot grow the people you manage because you are not giving them the opportunity; and (2) you cannot devote the time you need to coach the people you manage (as you are doing the work yourself)."

Learning to delegate is an essential skill and, when done as a habit, it becomes potent in helping managers achieve their required goals of getting the expected results and retaining and developing their people.

WHAT DELEGATION ISN'T

Sadly, many managers confuse giving people jobs to do as delegation. It isn't. That's task assignment. You will need to assign tasks to people as a manager but just be aware that all it is, task assignment. Tasks are things you would not normally do in your role. If you have come up through the ranks, you will have probably done them, but they are not things you are responsible for.

WHAT DELEGATION IS

Delegation is simply giving responsibility to someone else for something you are accountable for on a permanent or long-term basis.

Think about it. You probably are delegated work by your boss. Hopefully, they do it well too. But if you didn't delegate something else pretty quickly, you would reach overload. With only so many hours in a week, you would max out. The only solutions are not to do something altogether or to delegate.

The effective manager does a bit of both. They know what to stop doing as it adds little value and what to delegate to free up capacity.

As Donald Rumsfeld, former U.S. Secretary of Defense, said, "Don't be a bottleneck. If a matter is not a decision for the President or you, delegate it. Force responsibility down and out. Find problem areas, add structure and delegate. The pressure is to do the reverse. Resist it."

WHAT TO DELEGATE

This often confuses, especially when managers realise they shouldn't be assigning tasks. So what can we delegate?

There are four key things:

1. The production of key reports
2. Attendance or the running of some meetings

3. Compilation and delivery of some presentations
4. Some projects

Remember, the purpose of delegating these things is two-fold: to free up some of your time and as a development opportunity for that person. It's never about passing off work you don't like or can't be bothered doing.

HOW TO DELEGATE – THE A.W.A.I.R. MODEL

After years of delegating and trying different approaches, I created the following model. Other models are available.

Ask – influence not instruct
Why – state why you are asking them
Acceptance – ask for their acceptance
Information- what they need to know & authority
Result– be clear about the result required

ASK

By now, you will probably be aware that I'm going to say that the first step in delegating begins with asking whether you can trust something to them. We do this because the best managers rely on influence and not role power.

And that's the reason why ideally, this is the third habit to build after the first two. By now, if you have followed my process, you will have spent at least eleven weeks building your influence and emotional bank account through weekly one to ones and four weeks of only giving positive feedback.

It sounds like this:

"Natasha, I'd like your help, please."

It doesn't sound like:

"Hi Natasha, can I ask a favour?"or "Natasha, I need your help with something." Both those sound needy. You are not needy; this is a strategic choice for both your benefit.

WHY

The next step is to state why you are asking them. It's not enough to ask them because you want to free up some space or don't like a particular responsibility. It has to be more considered and strategic than that. If it's not, you'll find it will be picked up, and soon enough, people will stop saying yes when you ask. Then what do you do? Because if we are relying on influence and not position power, we have to respect their wishes. Don't resort to position power, and taking great chunks out of your emotional bank balance.

We need to do a bit of thinking and decide what we are going to delegate, and to who, based on the following four things:

- What they are **good** at
- What they **like** to do
- What they **need** to do
- What they **want** to do

ACCEPTANCE

The next bit is critical; that is where they get their acceptance. No acceptance, no go. You have to stand by your choice to use influence and not role power. Choose to go down the position power route at this point, and you undermine your integrity. If she declines, you can ask what her concerns are. Once you have listened, you might ask, "And if I can take some of those concerns away, would you be interested?"

If she says no, I'd say, "OK, no problem,I'll find someone else." Then walk away. Don't ask a second time or try and persuade.

Putting it together, it sounds like this:

"Hi Natasha, I'd like your help, please. I'd like you to take over the writing and delivery of the weekly finance report. I'm asking because I know how conscientious you are, and you are keen to take on more responsibility. Are you interested?"

Then wait for her response. They will often reply yes or ask for further information before agreeing to your request.

INFORMATION

This is where you share all the information they will need to take over the responsibility of completing the delegated work. You also delegate any required authority to get the job done.

RESULT

One of the most common objections managers share about delegating is that the work won't be as good as when they do it. Or that it takes up too much of their time dealing with questions and issues that they may as well do it themselves.

My answer is that those problems tend to lie with them not properly briefing someone. Yes, at the start, it will take a little time to ensure that the person is absolutely clear on the expectations about the following things: time, quality, budget, process, frequency etc., and that's on you as the delegator to make sure there is complete clarity.

Some managers forget that true delegation means the permanent or long-term handover of responsibility for doing something to another person. A few hours now will pay dividends in the medium to long term.

A word of caution!

Delegation may mean the permanent or long term handover of responsibility to do something to someone else. It does not include the handover of accountability. That always lies with you. Responsibility refers to someone's duty to carry out a task to completion; accountability generally refers to what happens after something has happened. As the manager that sits with you.

CHAPTER SUMMARY

Key takeaways:

1. Delegation buys you time
2. Delegation builds confidence and skills
3. Always ask and get buy-in

4. You delegate responsibility, not accountability

Questions to Reflect On

1. What's stopping me from delegating more?
2. How does this differ from my current approach to delegation?
3. What more could I delegate?
4. What would that do for my team and me?

8

Empower

"C*oaching is helping someone achieve something they didn't know they were capable of.*"
– Anthony Taylor

WHY EMPOWER?

One of the best examples of great coaching and the difference that it can make is the film The King's Speech, starring Colin Firth and Geoffrey Rush. If you haven't seen it, make sure you do. Rush plays an unorthodox speech therapist who helps Firth's King George VI character overcome a stammer and fear of public speaking as Britain faced war with Germany.

A coach's job is to move someone from where they are to where they want to be. Sometimes it's about helping them see what they can be rather than what they are. As a manager, you have to wear many hats, and a coach's hat is one. It doesn't mean that you have to be a trained coach or have one-hour, formal coaching sessions with your team members, although you can do both if you choose.

This is about having the mindset and creating the habit of taking a coaching approach. What does that mean? It means you stay out of the trap of giving advice and solutions every time you are asked a question. It means you remain curious and not judgmental. It means you are willing to help your direct reports become more than they are now. It means you help them think for themselves rather than coming to you for the answers all the time.

Do this, and it means you'll have a higher-performing team, you'll be seen as an influential leader and here's the best bit, you will end up with more time and fewer distractions.

Still not convinced? Google identified it as the number one skill in their Project Aristotle research based on observing more than 10,000 manager interactions.

Have you ever had a manager who took a coaching approach? Someone who subtly challenged you by asking you questions rather than just giving you answers. How often do you get coached by your boss?

WHAT STOPS YOU FROM COACHING?

This is a question I've asked hundreds of managers either in my management development programmes or in one to one coaching sessions. The four most common responses are:

- time,
- they feel it's inappropriate - "I'm not the touchy-feely type",
- they don't know if they have the skill sand tools
- and the fourth is they love giving advice!

Let's be honest; we all do it, don't we? It makes us feel good. It makes us feel knowledgeable and important, and it gives us a voice. And if someone takes our advice, we feel like we've made a difference.

So what stops you from taking a coaching approach with your team? Which of the four, or is it something else?

WHEN TO COACH

When we choose to adopt a coaching mindset, coaching opportunities become almost limitless. Think back over your last week. How often have your team come to you with problems they wanted you to solve? How often have you felt frustrated because they haven't spent much time thinking it through? What about times when they wanted general advice?

Have you got some underperforming people? What about those you are delegating things to? If you start delegating more, the opportunities to take a coaching approach increase.

Are there any other triggers that you can think of when a coaching mindset might be helpful? What about outside of work? When I was learning to coach back in 2006, I started to practice with family and friends, and as my kids grew up, with them too.

The more we practice being curious rather than giving advice and solutions, the more we naturally take a coaching approach.

HOW TO COACH

The coaching world loves a good model! You've possibly heard of GROW; then we have TGROW, CIGAR, OSKAR, STEPPA, MI etc. In truth, there are hundreds, and anyone can create a model according to what they are trying to achieve.

A coaching model is just a way to apply a framework or process to the conversation to move your 'client' from where they are to where they want to be. They can be adhered to rigidly but the best results come when they are applied flexibly.

To that end, I teach managers to use an adapted set of questions from Michael Bungay-Stanier's excellent book, The Coaching Habit.[15] I've put them in a simple model called COACH to help you help understand what role each of the nine, yes, just nine, questions plays in the conversation.

The COACH model stands for:

Context **O**bjective **A**cquire **C**larify **H**ow

Here are the nine questions in each section of the model.

Context

What's on your mind?
And what else?
What's the challenge here for you?

Objective
What do you want – what does success look like?

Acquire
What can you do?
What do you want from me?

Clarify
What are you committing to?
If you are saying yes to this, what are you saying NO to?

How
How do you want to follow up on this?

The thing to remember about this and any model is that it is not always linear. In fact, as I'll go on to show in an example, this is anything but linear. We start sequentially, then go back, then jump forward. It's just a framework for a conversation, and needs to be applied flexibly.

The following is a conversation adapted from a recent training course I delivered.

Adam: Hi, have you got a minute?
Mgr: Sure, what's on your mind?
Adam: Can I talk to you about the rota?
Mgr: OK, just the rota?
Adam: Yeah, we've got some problems with it

Mgr: OK, what else?

Adam: Well, actually it's Paula, she's not happy about it

Mgr: I see. What else?

Adam: Well, it's not just about the rota. I'm having some issues with her and her behaviour.

Mgr: Right. So what's the challenge here for you?

Adam: I'm finding it hard to manage her. She's rude and direct.

Mgr: OK, what else?

Adam: She's pretty challenging and asks lots of questions when I give her work to do rather than just doing it.

Mgr: Out of curiosity, what do you want?

Adam: Hmm, I guess I want her to change her attitude and stop asking so many questions.

Mgr: What else?

Adam: Err, I'm not sure. OK I want to stop feeling like she's challenging me all the time.

Mgr: Right. Just so I'm clear what do you want from me?

Adam: I'd like you to talk to her please and get her to stop

Mgr: What else?

Adam: Nothing, that's it.

Mgr: OK, assuming I agree to do that, and I'm not saying I will yet, what else could you do?

Adam: Well, I guess I could talk to her.

Mgr: And say what?

Adam: I could ask her why she's so short with me and why she keeps challenging me by asking lots of questions.

Mgr: And what's the real challenge here for you if you did that?

Adam: Probably managing my emotions and actually listening to what she says

Mgr: OK, that's insightful. What else?

Adam: Maybe to avoid jumping to conclusions?

Mgr: I see. I'm curious, what else?

Adam: Nothing that I can think of.

Mgr: OK so, now what do you want?

Adam: I want to have a chat with her to try and figure this out without falling out.

Mgr: OK great, so what will you do?

Adam: I'll arrange a meeting and explain why we are having the conversation and what I'm hoping to get from it.

Mgr: OK, good, what are you committing to?

Adam: I'll make sure I listen to what she says. I'll explain how it makes me feel and ask her how she's feeling before I tell her what I want.

Mgr: If you are going to do that, what will you not do?

Adam: I'll not make any assumptions or react to anything she says.

Mgr: Sounds like you have found a way forward. How do you want to follow up on this? Adam: Can I come back and tell you how it goes?

Mgr: Sure, I'd love to hear.

While a slightly contrived conversation, it's an illustration of how the model works; this is remarkably close to several real-world scenarios. Did you notice how fluidly the framework was applied? The manager kept going back and using the same two or three questions before allowing the conversation to move forward.

At no point did they offer any advice or suggestions. They stayed curious and non-judgmental and helped Adam figure out his own way forward for dealing with his colleague.

They also avoided framing a solution as a question. This is a common trap people fall into. In this case, it might have sounded like: "Have you tried asking why she does that?" That's a leading question and shuts down thinking when our objective as coaches is to get someone to open up their thoughts.

So there you have it, a simple framework for coaching anyone, anywhere, anytime using about nine questions. As with any skill, the more you practice it, the better you get.

CHAPTER SUMMARY

Key takeaways:

1. Coaching buys you time
2. Coaching builds confidence and skills
3. Use the simple and flexible COACH framework
4. Avoid leading questions - "Have you tried doing..?" "Could you try?"
5. It doesn't work if you don't use it

Questions to Reflect On

1. What's stopping me from coaching more?
2. And what else?
3. What's the challenge here for me?
4. What do I want and why?
5. What would success look like?
6. What can I do?
7. What am I committing to?
8. If I am saying yes to that, what am I saying no to?

9. How will I follow up?

9

Conclusion

I believe middle management is the most challenging job in business; we have to deal with what comes down from the top and absorb what comes up from below. We are the oil that keeps the engine running. Yet despite being so important, a great many receive little or no formal training.

That's an awful lot of good people who are trying to do their best with one hand tied behind their back.

I have shared the four fundamental habits for good person-centered management with this book. When you make these behaviours habits, you will notice a massive difference in your effectiveness and that of your team.

Given that the two responsibilities of all managers are to achieve the expected results and retain your people, you'll be well on your way.

Thank you for reading, and good luck with your career. Remember, management is a privilege, and it can also be fun.

References

1 Jan De Neve, 2018, Oxford Research Centre

2 https://www.gallup.com/workplace/232955/no-employee-benefit-no-one-talking.aspx

3 https://www.careeraddict.com/why-employees-quit

4 https://en.wikipedia.org/wiki/DunningKruger_effect

5 https://www.statista.com/statistics/738399/size-of-the-global-workplace-training-market/

6 https://weareworkforce.co.uk/2019/07/01/poor-management-costs-uk-business-84-million-a-year-new- rec-advice-on-how-to-turn-that-around/

7 https://www.mindsharepartners.org/post/why-50-of-millennial-and-75-of-gen-z-workers-have-left-jobs

8 Tips From The Top: How To Successfully Navigate Middle Management, 6JA Publishing, https://amzn. to/335ZlHK

9 https://www.gallup.com/workplace/247391/fixable-problem-costs-businesses-trillion.aspx

10 https://www.weforum.org/agenda/2021/11/what-is-the-great-resignation-and-what-can-we-learn-from- it/

11 https://en.wikipedia.org/wiki/Maslow%27s_hierarchy_of_needs

12 https://drive.google.com/file/d/1ItriTt_z0-wrgdaM9iyTEhK0HDYkDP8z/view?usp=sharing

13 Tips From The Top – The Secrets of How to Navigate Middle Management, https://amzn.to/346TGC0
14 The Advice Trap – Be Humble, Stay Curious And Change The Way You Lead Forever, https://amzn. to/3hwQNxn
15 The Coaching Habit – Say Less, Ask More, Page Two Publishing https://amzn.to/3sE3Nrx

About the Author

Anthony Taylor is the founder of ThreeFifty9, a consultancy dedicated to middle managers' professional and personal development. He is a multiple-author, professional keynote speaker, podcaster and executive coach of 16 years. Anthony has extensive experience building and leading teams in multiple sectors in the UK and internationally. He spent four years in the Caribbean, has twice been adrift at sea and been hung upside down from a fishing boat by some unhappy sailors. He now lives in land-locked Cheshire with his wife, children and Ed the dog

You can connect with me on:

https://www.threefifty9.com

https://twitter.com/AntTaylor72

Subscribe to my newsletter:

https://sendfox.com/anthony

Also by Anthony Taylor

Anthony writes about leadership, management and personal development.

Tips from the Top - The Secrets of How to Navigate Middle Management

This is a collection of interviews with 28 people who have raised to the top of the various professions and industries and how they got there.

"The problem with management books is they are written in management speak. Wonderfully this book captures, through a meander of thoughts, insights and reflections that being human and real is what it is all about." I. Anderson

Mental Toughness Metaphors - Stories to build resilience for parents, coaches, trainers and thinkers

If you liked Aesop's fables as a child then you'll love this collection of 20 short stories and metaphors.

"A great collection of short stories with powerful lessons, appropriate for all ages with added discussion questions and takeaway points. My family and I have really enjoyed exploring this book together and I'm sure it will prove beneficial for the classroom too." P Nixon

Printed in Great Britain
by Amazon

41847801R00046